CHRISTMAS
FROM HEAVEN

THE TRUE STORY OF THE BERLIN CANDY BOMBER

AS READ BY
TOM BROKAW

ILLUSTRATED BY
ROBERT T. BARRETT

WRITTEN FOR THE MORMON TABERNACLE CHOIR BY
DAVID T. WARNER

INCLUDES DVD OF TOM BROKAW WITH THE MORMON TABERNACLE CHOIR
AND ORCHESTRA AT TEMPLE SQUARE

SHADOW MOUNTAIN®

MORMON TABERNACLE CHOIR®

Historical photo credits: page 2 (top) C. H. Hewitt/British Imperial War Museum/public domain; page 4 (bottom) US Department of Agriculture/public domain; page 8 (top) US Navy National Museum of Naval Aviation/public domain; page 15 (bottom) USAF/public domain; page 20 USAF/public domain; all others courtesy Gail Halvorsen.

Text and DVD © 2013 Intellectual Reserve, Inc.

Illustrations © 2013 Robert Barrett

Art direction by Richard Erickson

Design by Sheryl Dickert Smith, Barry Hansen, and Shauna Gibby

Visit us at ShadowMountain.com

Library of Congress Cataloging-in-Publication Data

Brokaw, Tom, author.

   Christmas from heaven : the true story of the Berlin candy bomber / Tom Brokaw ; Illustrated by Robert T. Barrett.

     pages cm

   ISBN 978-1-60907-700-6 (hardbound w/ dvd : alk. paper)

1. Halvorsen, Gail S. 2. Berlin (Germany)—History—Blockade, 1948–1949. 3. United States. Air Force. Military Airlift Command—Biography.

4. Air pilots, Military—United States—Biography. I. Barrett, Robert, 1949– illustrator. II. Title.

   DD881.B7235 2013

   943'.1550874—dc23   2013019597

Printed in China   8/2020

RR Donnelley, Dongguan, China

10   9   8   7   6

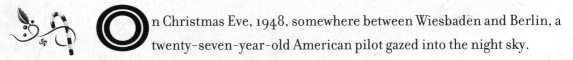

On Christmas Eve, 1948, somewhere between Wiesbaden and Berlin, a twenty-seven-year-old American pilot gazed into the night sky.

After World War II, Berlin was left in ruins.

A C-54 lands at Tempelhof.

◄ *Lt. Gail S. Halvorsen, 1944.*

The heavens were so full of stars, it seemed they would overflow and tumble to earth in a brilliant display of Christmas generosity and joy.

Hal, as he was known to his crew, wrapped his hands around the yoke of his C-54 cargo plane packed with 20,000 pounds of flour. "This is the real spirit of Christmas," he thought to himself as he guided his plane toward Tempelhof Air Base in West Berlin.

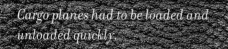

Cargo planes had to be loaded and unloaded quickly.

A cargo plane loaded with 100-pound sacks of flour.

When World War II had ended three years earlier, Germany and its capital city were divided between the Western allies and the Soviet Union. Then, in a grab for power, Stalin blocked ground transportation into the city. To preserve freedom and keep two and a half million West Berliners from starving, the United States and Britain began transporting food and other basic supplies by air.

Hal was one of hundreds of Americans who participated in the historic Berlin Airlift, dubbed "Operation Vittles."

That snowy Christmas Eve, as Hal radioed for clearance to land, his mind wandered back six months to the day that had changed his life. He had been standing at the end of the Tempelhof runway, taking home movies of arriving planes, when he noticed about thirty children on a grassy strip just beyond a barbed wire fence. In broken English, they asked about the planes, how much flour each one carried, and whether the airlift would continue. Although the children had been on meager rations, they were more concerned with freedom than with flour. They wanted what Hal had always had—the opportunity to pursue their dreams.

Lt. Halvorsen visits with German children standing behind a fence at the end of the Tempelhof runway.

For nearly an hour Hal answered their questions before saying good-bye. As he turned away, one question lingered in his mind: "What makes these kids different?" All over the world, children were known to beg candy from American servicemen. These children had little to eat, and no candy at all, yet they were grateful for what the airlift had given them and asked for nothing. Their gratitude melted Hal's heart.

German children peer through the fence at the end of Tempelhof runway.

C-47 cargo planes being unloaded at Tempelhof.

Lt. Halvorsen in Berlin.

Instinctively he wanted to give something back. Digging into his pockets, he found only two sticks of gum. "From little things come big things," his father used to say. A broad smile crossed Hal's boyish face. Giving so little to so many could cause a squabble, he reasoned. But a quiet voice within him urged him on.

Hal broke the gum into four pieces and passed it through the fence.

Without a word, the four children tore the gum wrappers into strips and passed them to the others. One by one, each small nose was pressed to the paper, breathing in the minty smell. Never had he seen such expressions of joy and wonder, even at Christmas.

German children await "Uncle Wiggly Wings."

As Hal watched in amazement, his mind raced. "If only I had more to give!" he thought. He had his own rations of gum and chocolate. Maybe his buddies would be willing to donate theirs. Just then another C-54 roared over his head and an idea formed in his mind. "I could drop candy from the air," he said to himself.

He quickly explained his plan to the children. When they asked how to recognize his plane, he remembered flying over the family farm back home.

"I'll wiggle my wings," he announced, spreading his long arms and waving them up and down. The children giggled with delight. "Just promise me you'll share the candy," he said. All heads nodded in agreement.

By the next day, Hal had secretly enlisted his crew to donate their rations and make parachutes from handkerchiefs. As Hal's plane approached the runway and the grass came into view, he wiggled his wings, and a knot of waiting children exploded, running and jumping in the air. With the precision of bombardiers, the airmen pushed the candy out the flare chute, and white canopies floated to earth. Thirty children ran with open arms to catch the treasures.

Candy parachutes are released from a C-54.

Lt. Halvorsen holding the first three parachutes to be dropped.

As Operation Little Vittles became more popular, donations of candy poured in from all over.

Hal and his buddies were as excited as the children. The thrill of giving was irresistible. Soon they were dropping parachutes every day—hundreds of them.

The press caught on, and reports went out. Mail for "Uncle Wiggly Wings" began piling up at Base Operations. Hal found himself standing before his superior, expecting to be court-martialed. But the colonel surprised him. "Halvorsen," he said, "General Tunner thinks it's a good idea."

Soon hundreds of airmen were donating rations. Operation Little Vittles quickly captured the imagination of people everywhere. Candy and handkerchiefs poured in from around the world. Hal became known as "The Candy Bomber" and "The Chocolate Pilot."

Across West Berlin, children gathered to catch the parachutes and share the candy with each other. And they sent hundreds of thank-you letters, like the one addressed to "Dear Onkl of the Heaven." Some included maps and instructions: "Fly along the big canal to the second bridge, turn right one block. I live in the bombed-out house on the corner. I'll be in the backyard every day at 2 P.M. Drop the chocolate there."

Day by day, the parachutes brought peace and the candy renewed hope. The children made friends of their former enemies, and their parents' hearts were softened. The wounds of war began to heal.

DEAR AMERICAN PILOTS.
THERE WAS MUCH JOY WHEN OUR TEACHER TOLD US THAT WE COULD VISIT THE AIR PORT TODAY. NIGHT AND DAY YOU BRING US FOOD AND COAL WITH YOUR PLAUNES. IF YOU WOULD NOT BRING US OUR FOOD THROUGH THE AIR WE ALL WOULD HAVE NOTHING TO EAT. I AN SURE THAT THERE WILL BE TROOBLE SOMETIMES AND SOME AMERICAN PILOTS HAVE LOST THEIR LIFES IN ORDER TO CARE FOR US. I THANK YOU VERY MUCH FOR YOUR HELP AND REMAIN WITH THE BEST WISHES FOR YOU

Inge Sobisch

Berlin-Schöneberg
Naumannstraße 7

Christine.

Bärbel
Helgert

By December, the Little Vittles operation had gathered eighteen tons of candy from American candy makers, and three more tons came in from private donors. The spirit of Christmas was descending on people everywhere, lifting them up in the joy of giving.

An old fire station became the Center for Operation Little Vittles in the United States. The center shipped tons of supplies donated by individuals and businesses.

Lt. Halvorsen with several candy-loaded parachutes.

West Berlin children watch an approaching cargo plane, hoping for a candy drop.

That Christmas Eve, the twenty-seven-year-old American pilot blinked back tears. The stars overhead could not be more beautiful than skies overflowing with parachutes, tumbling to earth in a brilliant display of Christmas generosity and joy.

Lt. Halvorsen with an armload of silk parachutes.

His father was right: "From little things come big things." Hal in his cockpit pulled back on the yoke as his wheels rolled onto the familiar runway. This is the real spirit of Christmas— to give whatever we have, no matter how small the gift.

In that moment Hal Halvorsen prayed for the courage to never give anything less.

THE CANDY BOMBER

Colonel Gail S. Halvorsen was born in Salt Lake City, Utah, and grew up on small farms in Utah and Idaho. He earned a private pilot license under the non-college Civilian Pilot Training program in September 1941, and then joined the Civil Air Patrol as a pilot. He joined the United States Army Air Corps in June 1942 and trained as a fighter pilot with the Royal Air Force. He then returned to the Army Air Corps and was assigned flight duty in foreign transport operations in the South Atlantic Theater.

Following the end of World War II, Russia laid siege to Berlin, cutting off the flow of food and supplies into the city. The blockade began in June 1948 and continued into May 1949. Gail Halvorsen was one of hundreds of US pilots used in a massive airlift to provide sustenance to the people of Germany. He became known as Uncle Wiggly Wings, the Chocolate Flyer, and the Berlin Candy Bomber.

His efforts made a substantial impact on the post-war perception of Americans among the German people. Since then, he has returned to Germany many times, including an assignment as commander of Tempelhof Air Base in western Berlin. In 1974 he was awarded the German Service Cross to the Order of Merit from the Federal Republic of Germany, one of Germany's highest awards. The Gail S. Halvorsen Elementary School at Rhein-Main Air Base in Frankfurt, Germany, was named in his honor. In 2013, Colonel Halvorsen was present when a secondary school in the Berlin suburb of Zehlendorf was also named in his honor. This marked the first time a school in Berlin has been named after a living namesake. He served in the US Air Force for thirty-one years, much of that time spent in research and development in the space program. After his Air Force career, he was assistant dean of student life at Brigham Young University from 1978 to 1988.

Col. Halvorsen married Alta Jolley of Zion National Park, Utah, in 1949. They are the parents of five children, twenty-four grandchildren, and forty-one great-grandchildren. Following Alta's death in January 1999, Gail married his high school sweetheart, Lorraine Pace. A member of The Church of Jesus Christ of Latter-day Saints, he has served in many leadership positions, including callings as a bishop, stake president, and high councilor. He and his wife Alta served LDS missions to England, Russia, and the Joseph Smith Memorial Building in Salt Lake City, Utah.

HOW TO MAKE A CANDY PARACHUTE

Materials required
1 sheet of tissue paper, 24" x 24"
2 pieces of string, approximately 48" long each
4 pieces of tape, about 2" long each
1 piece of candy

Assembly instructions
Tape the ends of one string to opposite corners of the tissue paper. Tape the ends of the second string to the remaining two corners.

Pull the strings together, bringing the four corners of the paper together, and find the middle of the strings. Tie an overhand knot in the middle of the strings, creating a small loop (see illustration). Attach candy to loop.

Hold parachute from the center top and drop.

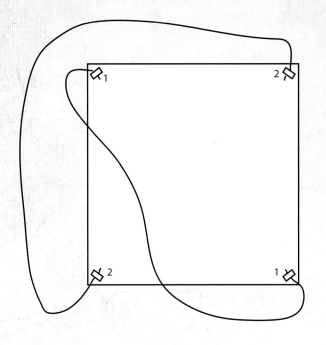

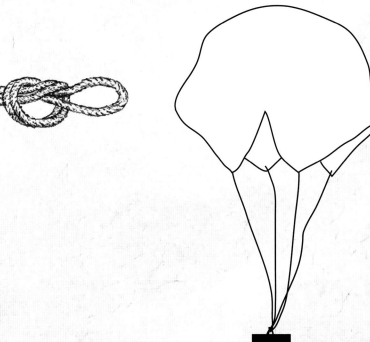

Photo by Ed Thompson; courtesy Mormon Tabernacle Choir.

EVERY DECEMBER, one of the many wonders of Christmas in Salt Lake City is the annual concert of the Mormon Tabernacle Choir and Orchestra at Temple Square, a Temple Square tradition for decades. Since the turn of the twenty-first century, these popular concerts have delighted live audiences of over 80,000 people each year in the LDS Conference Center, with millions more tuning in each year to *Christmas with the Mormon Tabernacle Choir* on PBS television. It is a full-scale production featuring world-class musicians, soloists, dancers, narrators, and music that leaves viewers in awe year after year.

Each concert has featured a special guest artist, including stage and screen star Angela Lansbury (2001); mezzo-soprano Frederica von Stade (2003); baritones Bryn Terfel (2003) and Nathan Gunn (2011); Broadway singer and actress Audra McDonald (2004); opera diva Renée Fleming (2005); Norwegian singing sensation Sissel (2006); the internationally acclaimed King's Singers (2007); Tony Award–winning soloist Brian Stokes Mitchell (2008); multiple Grammy Award–winner Natalie Cole (2009); *American Idol* finalist David Archuleta (2010); and British tenor Alfie Boe (2012). The remarkable talents of Emmy Award–winning actors Peter Graves (2004), Edward Herrmann (2008), and Jane Seymour (2011), plus British actors Michael York (2010),

and Claire Bloom (2005) have graced the stage, sharing memorable stories of the season. The esteemed list of featured guests also includes noted TV news anchorman Walter Cronkite (2002), two-time Pulitzer Prize–winning author David McCullough (2009), and famed broadcast journalist Tom Brokaw (2012).

The 360 members of the Mormon Tabernacle Choir represent men and women from many different backgrounds and professions and range in age from twenty-five to sixty. Their companion ensemble, the Orchestra at Temple Square, includes over 150 musicians who accompany the Choir on broadcasts, recordings, and tours. The combined forces—all serving as unpaid volunteers—reflect a medley of unique lives and experiences and are brought together by their love of performing and their faith.

The Mormon Tabernacle Choir has appeared at thirteen world's fairs and expositions, performed at the inaugurations of six US presidents, and sung for numerous worldwide telecasts and special events. Five of the Mormon Tabernacle Choir's recordings have achieved "gold record" and two have achieved "platinum record" status. One of the most notable was the Grammy Award–winning 1959 release of *The Battle Hymn of the Republic* with the Philadelphia Orchestra.

My best thanks
for the „Sky-Food".

Rose-Mary Fricke
Berlin-Schöneberg, Gustav-Müller-Platz 1
Berlin, 14ᵗᵉ okt. 1948.